True Colors

Emily Massicotte

BookLeaf Publishing

India | USA | UK

Presentation by *BookLeaf Publishing*

Web: www.bookleafpub.com

E-mail: info@bookleafpub.com

ISBN: 9789363312289

First edition 2024

This collection is dedicated to everyone who is still working on accepting their true colors. I hope these poems inspire you to embrace the hues that make you unique so that others may bask in your vibrant glow.

ACKNOWLEDGEMENT

Curating this collection of poems has been a rewarding journey for me, and it would not have been possible without #TheWriteAngle challenge presented by BookLeaf Publishing. This challenge came into my life at the perfect time, and I am incredibly grateful to have the opportunity to share my voice with the world.

Additionally, I would not have found the courage to share my poems without the undying support of my friends and family. Devesh, thank you for reading these poems with both a critical eye and an encouraging mind. You truly pushed this collection to the next level with your editorial expertise. Cordelia, not a day has gone by in which I haven't felt your love. You make me feel seen and accepted, and I couldn't have asked for a better friend to embark on this journey with. Thank you both for being the people who urge me to "learn from my mistakes." This collection paired with your kind words have finally encouraged me to try doing just that.

Ben, thank you for your honesty through this process. Your humor and directness never fails to ground me. Mom, thank you for letting me talk in circles for hours until I could finally make sense of the nonsensical world we live in. Your attention to detail is key and your insight helps me see every situation from a new perspective. And Dad, thank you for always encouraging my literary efforts. From late night proofreading sessions in Middle School to helping me proofread my first publication, you have always been there for me and I am eternally grateful for your encouragement and loving support.

Lastly, it feels fitting to acknowledge the people who inspired these poems. Though you will remain unnamed with the intention of keeping the past behind me, know that you each were a large part of this journey. Many of the experiences that birthed these poems were painful, both to live through and to write about, but nonetheless I can confidently say I would not be the successful person I am today without each and every one of you.

TABLE OF CONTENTS

My Poems Are Nothing Special

I'm no Dickinson or Gordon or Frost
My lines just aren't as clever as the Bard's

I don't even follow a rhyme scheme
Or a meter or a template

My punctuation and capitalization are sporadic
And I rarely bother to count my syllables

I just write the words that come to me
And trust the simple process

The inconsistency is uneasy
And sometimes it makes me want to quit

But within each new poem I manage to learn
Something about me, them, or even you

With a pencil to the paper
My thoughts become so clear

And the confusing string of consciousness simply flows
Into broken lines that reveal the true joys and challenges in life

So I hope in reading this collection
You have grace

Try to search for the soul in each piece
Hiding beneath the battered surface

If you dig deep enough you just might find
A shining piece of humanity to carry with you

As you carry on your day

Inner Yarn

My thoughts are a tangled ball of yarn
Shoved in the back of my mind
And every day I crochet a new line of consciousness…

Until I tug at the yarn with no success

It is then and only then that I work through the tangles
Unknotting just enough to continue weaving my ideas

I stitch and stitch, crocheting line after line until I am again
Forced to stop and untangle that pesky string

The cycle is endless, and the knots in my thoughts plague me at the
Worst moments
Leaving me with anxiety ridden days and sleepless nights

It's only when telling stories that I feel truly in control

When I string a tale together, it strengthens my inner yarn
It grows and flows for hours, creating complex patterns with ease

Until at last a beautiful blanket of understanding is completed
And I have a powerful story to share with the world

The Importance of Stories

3

I am always telling stories.

Sometimes I invent them,
Weaving intricate yarns for young children
Or selling heartbroken teens on romanticized fairytales.

Other times I discover them within myself.
Memories hide themselves in my stories,
Disguised as my thoughts, feelings, and reactions.

But most importantly, I observe the stories I write.
I take note of those around me and recount the tales
That haven't yet had the chance to shine.

I am constantly observing and telling new stories
In hopes that someday
Everyone can look at my work with admiration
Using it as both a window into other's lives
And as a mirror reflecting their own.

As a storyteller I not only create this looking glass
But I polish it, ensuring every story stays alive
So multiple generations may gaze upon my work and see

Themselves
Their family
Their ancestors
Their friends
Their neighbors
Their coworkers

For though each story is unique, the core of my tales apply to all,
Encouraging us to observe and listen to other stories
With clear, perceptive minds and open, loving hearts.

Fleeting Friendships

The best friends are sent into your life with a purpose
A specific goal to unite you both

They may be there to make you laugh
Or maybe it's time for a really good cry
They could provide comfort when you start to lose hope
Or perhaps they're there to push you towards your next adventure

No matter their true purpose
They ensure you aren't alone in the dark
As you begin to embrace your authentic self
The comfort they provide is unmatched

Even if it's fleeting

For at the end of the mission
You must find a reason to part
As the hues of your soul change
And you have new needs to be met

But this change doesn't outweigh the good they've done for you
And you'll still miss them when their song is on the radio
You'll still long for their light on the darkest days
But at least you can be grateful they ever warmed your life at all

Them

Your eyes
flutter open
and see…
Black.
A hole.
An abyss
waiting
to
swallow
you.
You try to
breathe
but the
sticky
darkness
gets caught in
your throat.
So much
fear.
Such vast
darkness.
Must find
light.
Must get
air.
Your hands
claw at the
darkness
searching for
any way
out.
Suddenly you feel

Them.

Their soft hands and reassuring smile

"Everything will be OK"

At last the air floods your lungs and light begins to shine.
Until the audience fades into view
and your pulse
starts racing
again.
And suddenly
you long
for the
suffocating
abyss.
You hope to
cling to
Their
soft silhouette
until the
darkness
finds you and
swallows
your fears.
But They have
vanished.
Your eyes
frantically
search
until at last
you spot
Their
sapphire eyes gazing intently from high in the room.
They wink and nod telling you to go on.
Your face relaxes into a helpless smile as if to say

"Thanks"

They vanish again, but this time you open your mouth
letting your inner song break out at long
long last.

Dreams in a Stare

8

I feel so respected when I see
your soulful eyes smiling at me

Every note you sing is a promise
Every line you say is a guarantee

And when our stares collide I know I too will someday be
brave enough to take the stage, standing tall, proud, and free

With your confident composure you have proven to me
that my dreams can become a reality

The Gift

I nudge the present toward you
Brightly colored, neatly wrapped

I watch as your delicate fingers
Clumsily fiddle with the ribbon

I bite my lip as you tear into the paper
Awaiting your reaction with an anxious gaze

You begin to chuckle
My heart skips a beat

Do you like it?
Do you like me?

My doubts are quickly settled
As you wrap me in a hug

My fears melt away in your warm embrace
And I relax, snuggling in and smiling

"Thank you" I whisper
"This is the best gift of all"

The Power of Rainbows

You are my rainbow
In every storm I can look out and find
Your magnificent colors keeping me dry

Your vibrant red
Teaching me that controlled rage can be
Powerful when used deliberately

Your rusty orange
Showing me that everyone has their
Imperfect shade

Your bright yellow
Giving me a reason to get up every day
With a smile on my face

Your soft green
Showering me with hope and gratitude even when I feel
Unworthy of such high praise

Your deep blue
Proving that every problem is less daunting
In the face of joyous laughter

Your mysterious purple
Reminding me to always expect the unexpected

You've inspired me to be a rainbow too
To shield against my own rain clouds
And help others stay dry

I'm not ready to show my true colors yet
But when I finally do
Know that every color
Every delicate hue
Was once inspired directly by you

My True Colors

I feel like I'm hiding my true colors.

Even when my confidence spikes
Even when I know the best thing I can do is be "me"

I feel like I'm hiding my true colors.

And the doubt grows in the darkness
Feeding on my muted hues
Suffocating my vibrant shades
Until they are nothing more than a fading memory

When I see people holding space
Yearning to meet "me"
I freeze
What if the "me" they want to see is not the real me
But a "me" they've created in their minds?

For the real me is made of diverse shades
That hide deep in the darkness
And it's scary to be vulnerable
It's scary to let them see the light of day
So even though I know they are the best part of me

I will continue to hide my true colors.

Finding My Path

It's hard to feel at home in your skin
when everyone is already in love
with the version of you
they've created in their heads.

They seem to know me better than I know myself
analyzing my thoughts and feelings with a daunting certainty
until it feels easier to follow the path they've laid upon my feet
than to embark on my own journey.

Because if I get lost while following their map
at least I have the faulty trailblazer to blame
and if I am misled by my own brain, then I have no choice
but to take the fall.

Girls Turn Mean

They start as friends who share the same jokes
Until one becomes a threat

Maybe she's pulled one too many guys
Perhaps her slender figure is the root of their insecurity

And the longer she shines brightly as herself
The more harmful their jealous remarks become

Until there is nothing left of her
As she clings to the bottom rung of the social ladder

Instead of offering a helping hand
The rest of the girls climb over her
Clawing their way to success
Undercutting everyone who stands between them and their dreams

And that's how girls turn mean

But it's not all their fault
We push them to the edge
Until they think it's kill or be killed
And they have no choice but to attack their prey
Letting a goat take the fall for their actions
While they ride the wave to success

The meanest girls are just good at the game
we taught them they must play to survive

And that's really how girls turn mean

Fireworks

It's never truly quiet

Not in my mind.

There's always some melody floating by

Or a moment to obsess over endlessly
until even its sharp edges are worn into a smooth shine

Or a clever comeback that appears moments too late
as its untapped potential flickers and fades

Sometimes there's an insult to internalize

Some intrusive thought that has taken hold
until it tears me limb from limb

It can feel so bleak. So dark.

But it's never truly dark

Not in my mind.

There are always some colors exploding

A fiery red warms my soul
with dancing flames

A comforting yellow paints
daisies and daffodils on my eyelids

And a chilling blue creates
a calming ocean scene

The colors blend together
to drown out the darkness

Like warm fireworks that light up the night sky
until at last it is bright as day

Finding Your Voice

Your pulse quickens.
Your hands shake.
You choke on the air
you force yourself to swallow.

This is your last chance to run.

You can pretend you heard nothing,
pretend their harsh words
didn't sting as you hide
the deep pain you're in.

You can spare yourself
from the humiliation,
from the vulnerability.

But you know what you must do.

You clench your fists
and open your mouth,
letting your truth flow fiercely out.

At first your words are met with
simple scared silence
as others look to you with
uncertain eyes.

But you continue to tell your story,
urging them to join you,
to bravely step up and tell their stories too.

At last you can feel their uneasy support,
hoping you can make this right.
A wave of relief washes through the crowd
as everyone realizes they aren't in this alone.

With their trust propelling you,
you step forward deliberately
finally feeling strong enough

To speak.

About love.
Against hate.
About tolerance.
Against violence.
About jealousy.
Against spite.

You step back as their faces relax,
melting into soft smiles that
thank you for your courage.

You bask in their gratitude, soaking up their silent praise
until you too are proud of your actions
and confident, for once, that you did the right thing.

"Only the Death of Me"
(A poem inspired by "doomsday"
by Lizzy McAlpine)

She lay in her icy coffin
balanced atop a hastily dug grave
the lid slightly ajar.
Her hands gripped a wilting bouquet of flowers
as if they were the only thing
connecting her to the land of the living.
Her large, white gown and
perfectly pinned curls gave her the look
of a happy bride waiting patiently for her
Prince Charming to rescue her.

But in her comatose state,
there was no hope for a happy ending.
All color had drained from her face
because her Prince Charming
was the one who dug her grave.
And now she lay in her cold coffin,
accepting her fate and waiting for
her Prince to come and seal the deal.

But her Prince could not be bothered
to put her swiftly out of her misery.
Instead, he spent the days digging more graves.
One quickly turned to ten,
which then multiplied into a hundred
until hundreds of thousands of
empty graves surrounded her.

Still, her Prince stubbornly avoided her plot.
He just appeared with the harsh morning light
and dug until the first star appeared
in the dark blanket of midnight.

Then, he stabbed his shovel into that day's dirt
and stared longingly at the sky
with a look of contemplation,
or perhaps that was avoidance.

And then, without warning,
he vanished as quickly as he had appeared hours earlier,
and the only sign of life was the shovel that
slowly leaned until gravity overcame it
and it crashed to the ground.

As if he was summoned by the shovel's drawn-out demise,
her Prince appeared again to snatch his tool
and start digging yet another grave.
The cycle continued through the seasons,
and through it all she lay in her coffin, waiting
for the day her Prince would finally end things.

Instead, he dug.
He dug despite the summer heat,
into the breeze of September,
and through the chill of October.
He did not give in to the
temptation of her still beauty
until the last leaves succumbed
to the luring pull of gravity.

When at last every leaf rested
upon the upturned Earth,
a chill whizzed through the air.
A chill so sharp it split
the metal handle of his shovel
and bit at his ears and fingers and toes.
And in that moment, he finally noticed her,
glowing in her coffin.

Everything about her radiated
a kind and warm forgiveness,
a sharp contrast to the icy field
that surrounded him.

He eyed her longingly
for several long moments
until he could bear it no longer.

Like a zombie, he staggered toward her,
his arms outstretched,
craving her warmth.
His limbs longed to hold her,
his lips longed to kiss her,
and his soul longed to save her.

But it was too late.
By the time he reached the coffin,
the cold had overcome him,
and he collapsed upon it in a heap,
knocking the lid into place.
With a fatal click,
her fate was sealed,
and gravity slid her coffin
into the grave it had resisted
for so many months.

Her Prince watched in disbelief,
refusing to believe he had been
the final nail in her coffin.
Yet there she was,
forever at rest six feet in the ground.
Her coffin seemed to glow
brighter in response,
as if all the anguish,
sorrow,
guilt,
and regret
that had been plaguing her
through the seasons
had transferred to her Prince
and she was relieved
to finally be laid to rest.

The glow persisted,
pulsing vibrantly around the field.
Without warning, she appeared above land once again
in a ghostly glory.
Her muted white dress had transformed
into a modest sundress full of vibrant colors,
her childish grin had returned a rosy blush to her cheeks,
and her bouquet was full of life once more,
braided carefully into her shimmering hair to form
a powerful crown.
And though her body was buried, her soul at last seemed free.

She glanced at her Prince,
crumpled in a hopeless heap,
chained by gravity to the freshly dug Earth
like an unfortunate prisoner awaiting his fate.
Despite everything he put her through,
all the pain and confusion she grappled with for months,
she took pity on her poor Prince and
bestowed one final kiss on his cold lips.

Her kiss rippled through his body,
and in an instant,
he was gone again,
at last one with the very Earth
he dedicated his life to destroying.

She sighed to herself,
letting a fistful of the upturned Earth
slip through her fingers.
And then, without warning,
she zipped into the night sky,
giggling and twirling like never before
until she was part of the magical midnight blanket,
just a twinkling star freed from the shackles of gravity and reality.

And just like that, the stubborn shattered shovel was
the only reminder of life in the field.
That is until the next girl appeared and lay in an icy coffin

of her own.

Unanswered Questions

Missing your lips and their soft tender touch
Were we ever in love or was that just lust?

Rememb'ring your eyes myster'ous and free
Were you thinking of her while looking at me?

Longing to clutch your hand tightly in mine
Was this a true love or a fun waste of time?

Last Thanks

I'm half expecting you to call
Not to apologize
But to simply show up for me
One last time

I want you to tell me you're proud
With a celebratory hug

This is the last win I credit to you
Before I'm allowed to thrive on my own

I hope you wake up tomorrow
Before it's finally too late
And dial my number without a second thought
So I can give you my last thanks

The Fine Print

25

They warn me to
  "learn from my mistakes" when talking about you

But after all this time I simply don't think
  "mistake" rings true

Perhaps timing was wrong
Perhaps we ruffled feathers

But even with all that in mind I don't see this as
  "better"

With you I was happy
Without you I'm just lost

Who knew falling in love comes with hidden
  "rules" in the fine print?

Love and Stormy Seas

Love is the most fleeting emotion
Like the salty air on a beach it rushes over you all at once
Hitting your senses like a refreshing balm
Coating your skin in a tender mist
And lulling your thoughts to sleep with a quiet pulse

But if you stay in the salty breeze for too long
The air begins to stale
Your skin starts to prune and burn
Your thoughts eventually break through the seawall
And seeds of doubt are planted in the cracks

The roots grow stronger until they explode
And the beachy balm becomes a bomb
Igniting a howling storm

Sand whips at your skin and salt stings your eyes
The ocean breeze rages until it finally drives you away
For few are strong enough to stick out the violent attacks
Until at last the salty balm returns
And they can kick up their feet and relax

As for me I tend to be leading the cowardly flee
As soon as the storm starts roaring
And the doubt creeps in
I march to another beach and feel free
Until the wind once again decides to turn on me

I've been stuck in this constant loop for as long as I can remember
And I worry I'll never be brave enough
To stick out the storm and finally see a rainbow
I worry the violent winds might destroy
The parts of the beach I cherish the most
And the calm that returns will pale
In comparison to what I once had

These worries haunt my dreams each night
As I ponder the effects of love
Do I have the blind faith it takes to stick out the storm?
Will I ever be brave enough to stay in love?

It Will Happen.

even though the blank screen haunts your dreams
and the waiting gnaws at your soul
destroying you from the inside out

know that It Will Happen.

the notification will appear
and you'll bite your lip to keep from
screaming
and crying
and shouting

you'll open the message with shaking fingers
you'll squeeze your eyes shut
and breathe to calm your racing heart

at last you will have the courage to peek
and you'll see that fateful word
the word that has the power to change everything

"Congratulations"

It Will Happen.

Opening the Door

28

I hear the cacophony of voices
before entering the room.
My hand lingers on the handle.

It's my last chance to run,
to find my own quiet corner to sink into
until the voices in my head are all that remain.

But instead I take a deep breath and slowly turn the key.
Ready to embrace what lies behind the door with confidence.
Ready to start the next chapter with an open Hartt.

The Truth About My Mane

My hair is long, messy, and unkempt.
It begs to be curly, but I silence its frizzy cries
by raking a plastic comb though its rebellious snarls.
I brush and brush until the knots are gone
and my hair becomes a lion's mane.
Though Simba can easily rock a teased mane,
an 18-year-old trying to survive college simply cannot.

I got so frustrated with my Lion King hair that
I accidentally made myself a meerkat.
When I go without washing it for a few days
the roots become greasy until I look
like Timon after falling in the watering hole.
But when I brush it, the grease spreads
down to the tip of each strand and
persuades them to stay straight.
I used to hate the feeling of grease matting my hair to my head
but I eventually learned to embrace it.
That's when my hair looks the straightest after all
and straight hair is the only acceptable style.
Everything else, from natural curls to beachy waves,
draws unnecessary attention to yourself,
and everyone knows that the only way to
survive in this society is to keep a low profile.
Like prey in the Savannah, the best plan is always
the one that allows you to blend in.
So I forfeited hygiene in favor of greasy hair.

My mom hates the drowned-meerkat style.
She wishes I would embrace my natural curls
and feel comfortable in my own skin.
I see where she's coming from.
I see how hiding behind a matted mess isn't fooling anyone.
I'm sure people can see right through my straight facade.

But my mom grew up in the 80s.
Puffy hair was a new, quirky trend.
She just doesn't understand the stares
(and glares)
that would accompany fluffy locks of gorgeous curls.

I do wear my hair curly sometimes,
but only when I'm around people I truly trust.
And it's not like I sport my natural curls.
I take each strand and manipulate it
into a canned curl that others can gawk at and compliment.
I twist my hair into a forced wave with a heated wand
until I feel like Simba pretending to be King.
It is just another way of hiding my true self after all.

I do love the way my hair looks when it's curled
even when the curls are just another artificial piece
of an elaborate game of dress-up.
But slowly burning the pieces every day is not fair to my hair
so I stick with my frizz and grease.

Sometimes, I secretly let my natural curls shine through.
I sneak products into my bathroom
and scrunch them in late at night.
And in the moment, it feels so freeing.
Even though the hour of intense care makes
my arms ache and my neck stiff
it's all worth it to see my voluminous curls smiling back at me.
Naturally, the curls are unpredictable.
They twist into different patterns with each new experiment
and I secretly love and embrace each individual look.
I sneak out of the bathroom and stay up for hours,
my crown of curls putting me into a contagiously good mood.

But when the morning comes around,
I take the brush and stubbornly rake it
through the free and luscious curls
until it returns to a static mane of frizz impossible to tame.

My mom has seen my curly hair some mornings
before the strands have met the pointed teeth of my plastic comb.
Though she's never said anything out loud,
her eyes beg me to embrace my hair,
willing me to wear it the way that feels best to me.
Though she won't ever understand how hard it is
to embrace my inner curly girl,
my mom supports me nonetheless.
Like my own personal Mufasa looking down on me,
she tries to protect my innocence
from the horrors of the world
as I search for the bravery
to rock my natural curls.

When the time is right,
I know she'll give me a big, proud squeeze,
thankful to be rid of my meerkat grease and mane of frizz.
But until then, she waits patiently in the background,
occasionally smiling softly at my perfect crown of curls,
as if to say

"You are beautiful"

And for now, that's all the support I need.